Hands-On STEAM
Learning Fun Workbook

Copyright © 2020 by Highlights for Children. All rights reserved.
Reproduction of these pages is permitted for classroom use only. Otherwise, no part of this book may be copied or reproduced without written permission of the publisher.

For information about permission to reproduce selections from this book for an entire school or school district, please contact permissions@highlights.com.

Published by Highlights Learning • 815 Church Street • Honesdale, Pennsylvania 18431
ISBN: 978-1-64472-187-2
Mfg. 10/2020
Printed in Madison, WI, USA
First edition
10 9 8 7 6 5 4 3

For assistance in the preparation of this book, the editors would like to thank:
Vanessa Maldonado, MSEd; MS Literacy Ed. K–12; Reading/LA Consultant Cert.; K–5 Literacy Instructional Coach
Kristin Ward, MS Curriculum, Instruction, and Assessment; K–5 Mathematics Instructional Coach
Jump Start Press, Inc.

Push or Pull?

Circle the pictures that show pushing. Cross off the pictures that show pulling.

You push objects away. You pull them closer.

TALK ABOUT IT!
What are some things you pull? What are some things you push?

Physical Science: Force and Motion

Work and Play

We pull and push things when we work. The boy is pulling a rake. We pull and push things when we play. The girl is pushing a big snowball.

How do you push or pull when you work or play? Draw a picture of yourself pushing or pulling.

Physical Science: Force and Motion

Move It!

Pushing and pulling make things move. Look at the pictures. Who is moving what? Draw lines to match.

> A little push can move **light** things. But you need a big push to move **heavy** things.

Physical Science: Force and Motion

Pull Hard!

The animals are playing tug-of-war. Who do you think will win? Find the **8** objects in this Hidden Pictures puzzle. Then color the scene.

Tug-of-war is a fun game to play with friends. What games do you like to play?

- envelope
- pencil
- magnet
- fishhook
- hamburger
- heart
- banana
- shovel

Physical Science: Force and Motion

Investigate: Pushing Is a Force

Air and water can push and pull, too. You can use air or water to push a ball without touching it.

YOU NEED:
- table-tennis ball
- pan half-filled with water
- turkey baster

Force is a push or a pull that happens when 2 objects interact.

1. Put the ball on the water. Blow on the ball. Make it move.
2. Puff lightly on the ball. What happens?
3. Blow harder on the ball. What happens?
4. Fill the turkey baster with water. Squeeze the water out next to the ball. What happens? Why?

TALK ABOUT IT!
- Which push—your breath or the water—has more force? How can you tell?
- Can you think of ways that air and water push and pull things in nature?

Physical Science: Force and Motion

Investigate: Fast, Slow, Stop, Go

Design a path for a ball.

YOU NEED:
- blocks
- ball

1. Use blocks to make walls for the path.
2. Set up some blocks to make the ball turn.
3. Make towers of blocks.
4. Push the ball toward the towers of blocks. What happens?

TALK ABOUT IT!
- How did you plan your path for the ball? Did the ball go where you wanted it to?
- What will happen if you change how hard you push the ball? How can you find out?
- Do the sizes of the blocks in the tower matter? Does the size of the ball matter? Try different sizes and see what happens!

Physical Science: Force and Motion

Create:
Puppet Pulls

Make a puppet that moves when you pull on strings.

YOU NEED:
- 2 pieces of string
- a stuffed animal with floppy arms

1. Tie a string around each arm of the stuffed animal.
2. Stand up. Hold the other end of each string.
3. Pull up to make the arms move. What happens if you pull quickly? What happens if you pull slowly?
4. Make the animal wave to a friend.

TALK ABOUT IT!
What other toys use strings to move?

A puppet that moves with strings is called a **marionette**.

Find the 2 sock monkeys that match exactly.

Physical Science: Force and Motion

Sun Power

The sun shines on Earth. It heats everything on Earth's surface. It melts snow and ice. How do you feel when the sun shines on you?

Ice is frozen water. It melts in the sun. It turns into liquid water.

These pictures of a melting ice pop are out of order. Can you number them 1, 2, and 3 to show what happened first, second, and third?

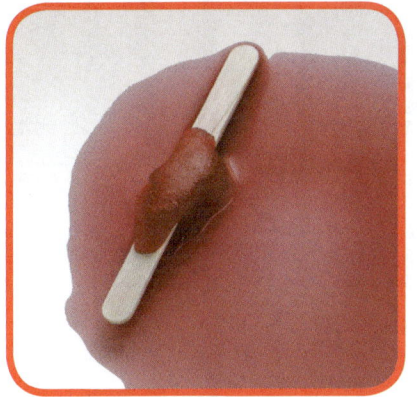  

Physical Science: Energy and the Effects of the Sun

Sun and Shade

You can cool off on a hot, sunny day by finding a shady spot. Circle the people keeping cool in the shade.

Sand on a beach warms up faster than ocean water does.

TALK ABOUT IT!
- What is your favorite way to keep cool on a hot day?
- What would you like to do if you were at this beach?
- Would the beach be warmer or cooler at night? Why?

Hot and Cold

Have you ever walked on hot sand in bare feet? The sun can make Earth's surface very hot! The surface is cooler when there is less sunshine.

The sand is hot. The lizard stands on just two feet at a time. This helps the lizard keep cool.

The rock is cold. The goose stands on just one foot at a time. This helps the goose keep warm.

TALK ABOUT IT!

A goose's feathers trap body heat. This helps the goose keep warm in winter months.
- What do you wear to keep warm in cold weather?
- What do you wear on a hot day to keep cool?

Draw lines to match each pair of flip-flops.

Physical Science: Energy and the Effects of the Sun

Investigate: Warming Up

How quickly do different parts of Earth's surface heat up?

YOU NEED:
- 3 pie pans
- light-colored sand
- dry potting soil
- room-temperature water
- a sunny spot

Dark colors soak up, or **absorb**, more light than pale colors do.

1. Fill one pie pan with sand, one with soil, and one with water.
2. Use your finger to touch the contents of each pan. Think about how it feels. Is it cool or warm?
3. Put the pans in a sunny spot. Leave them there for 30 minutes. Predict which ones will get warmer quickly.
4. Touch what is in each pan again. Which ones feel much warmer? Do any still feel cool?

sand

soil

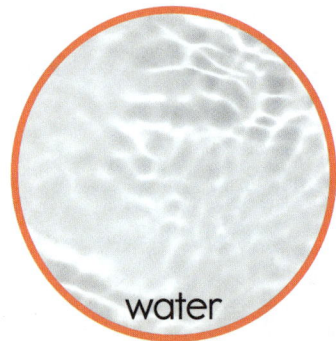
water

TALK ABOUT IT!
- Was your prediction correct? Why do you think the materials warmed up the way they did? What might happen if you leave them in sunlight all day?
- Think about what you wear on a hot, sunny day. How could you test to find out if a dark shirt or a light shirt gets warmer on a sunny day?

Invent:
Keep Your Cool!

Look at these children. How are they keeping cool on a sunny day?

Design a structure that could slow down how quickly an ice cube melts in the sun. Use only things you can find in your home or yard.

1. Make a plan. Draw a picture that shows the design of your structure.
2. Follow your plan to make the structure.
3. Share your structure with an adult. Tell how the shelter would keep the ice cube cool on a sunny day.
4. Test your structure using a real ice cube on a sunny day. What happened? Think about ways you might improve your design.

TALK ABOUT IT!
- Why do you think blocking sunlight keeps something cool?
- Could your structure stop the ice cube from melting at all? Why or why not?
- What could you use to shade yourself in the sunlight?

Physical Science: Energy and the Effects of the Sun

Time to Eat

You need food to live and grow. Animals do, too. Match each animal with the food that it eats.

What do you like to eat? Draw it on the plate.

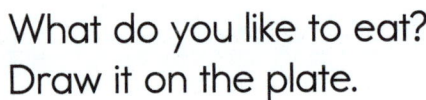

TALK ABOUT IT!
- Why do you think different animals eat different kinds of food?
- Where do animals find their food?
- What foods do animals eat that people eat, too?

Green and Growing

Circle the things that plants need to live and grow. Cross off the things they do not need.

Many kinds of animals eat plants. People eat plants, too.

TALK ABOUT IT!
- What happens to a plant that does not get what it needs to live and grow?
- Where have you seen plants growing?
- What kinds of plants have you seen?
- What kind of plant would you like to grow?

Life Science: Needs of Living Things

Grow, Seeds, Grow!

Different kinds of seeds grow into different kinds of plants. Follow the paths to find out which plant grew from which seed.

Plants need air, soil, water, and light to grow.

TALK ABOUT IT!
- Why do plants make seeds?
- What kinds of seeds have you seen in fruits and vegetables from the store?
- Describe how you would plant a garden with seeds.

Life Science: Needs of Living Things

Wild Wonders

These people are looking at wild animals and plants. See if you can find the 12 objects in this Hidden Pictures puzzle.

A place where animals and plants live in the wild is called their habitat.

- flashlight
- vase
- magnifying glass
- light bulb
- bowling pin
- paper clip
- four-leaf clover
- belt
- seal
- wishbone
- ladder
- glove

TALK ABOUT IT!
- What animals can you see in the picture? What are the different animals doing? What kinds of food do you think they can find here?
- Do the plants have everything they need to live and grow?

Create:
Paint and Plant

Paint pots. Then plant some seeds and watch them grow.

> **YOU NEED:**
> • small terra-cotta pots and saucers • acrylic paint
> • paintbrushes • potting soil • bean or squash seeds

1. Paint the pots. Let them dry.
2. Put soil into each pot.
3. Use your finger to poke a hole in each pot's soil.
4. Drop a seed into each hole. Cover it with soil.
5. Put your pots in a sunny place that does not get too hot.
6. Water your plants every day. Place saucers under the pots to catch extra water.

TALK ABOUT IT!
- What happens to the seeds?
- Why must you water the plants?
- Why do the plants need sunlight?
- Will plants grow without water? What about without sunlight? How can you test to find out?

Life Science: Needs of Living Things

Plant Power

These trees burned in a forest fire. But new plants are growing all around them. Over time, plants will change the land.

TALK ABOUT IT!
- What kinds of plants can you see in the pictures on this page?
- What do plants need to grow?
- What did the log in the picture below used to be?

This family is hiking in a forest that has grown back. Can you find the **7** objects in this Hidden Pictures puzzle?

lemon

spoon

ear of corn

iron

closed umbrella

broccoli

belt

Life and Earth Science: Plants and Animals Change Their Environments

Acorns to Oaks

A big oak tree can grow about 10,000 acorns in one year!

Oak trees drop acorns in the fall. Squirrels bury acorns to store food for the winter. Some acorns they forget to dig up will grow into new trees.

These squirrels are racing to gather nuts. Follow the paths to help each squirrel find a nut.

TALK ABOUT IT!
- Why do squirrels have to gather nuts and store them for the winter?
- How many nuts do you think they need to store?
- Do you store anything at home? Explain.

Investigate: Busy as a Beaver

No pond? No problem! A beaver can make its own pond to live in.

First, the beaver chews on trees to cut them down.

Then the beaver uses logs and sticks from the trees to make a dam. The dam holds in water. A pond forms.

TALK ABOUT IT!
- How do the beavers change the land?
- What other animals do you think will use the pond, too?
- What will happen if the dam breaks? What do you think the beavers will do if that happens?

Now it's your turn. Change the way water flows, like beavers do!

YOU NEED:
- shallow pan • dirt • small block • measuring cup • water • sticks

1. Spread a layer of dirt in a shallow pan. Place the pan on a surface with one end raised by a small block.
2. Pour a cup of water in one spot on the high end of the pan. Watch where the water goes.
3. Place sticks and rocks in the pan.
4. Pour another cup of water in the same spot as step 2. Watch where the water goes. Did the water take the same path? Why or why not?

Life and Earth Science: Plants and Animals Change Their Environments

At Home in Holes

Some animals make holes to live in. Circle the animals that make holes. Cross off the animals that do not make holes.

All the living and nonliving things in an area make up an animal's **environment**.

TALK ABOUT IT!
- Can you think of other animals that live in holes?
- Describe the environment that you live in.
- Describe an environment that you have visited.

TRY THIS!
Take a walk through your yard or in a park. Look for holes in the ground or in the trees. What animals might live in the holes? Why do you think they need to live in holes?

Life and Earth Science: Plants and Animals Change Their Environments

Create: Set Up a Scene

Change a box into a mini natural world!

> **YOU NEED:**
> • paper   • crayons or markers   • glue or tape
> • shoebox   • scissors
> • pebbles, sticks, and other natural objects

1. Think of a place where plants and animals live.
2. Draw plants that live in the place you chose. Glue or tape your drawings inside the box on its sides and back.
3. Draw animals that live in the place you chose. Cut them out. Place them in your scene.
4. Add pebbles and other natural objects to the scene. Glue them inside the box.

TALK ABOUT IT!
- What do the animals in your scene eat? Where do they sleep?
- Could the animals live in a different environment? What about the plants?
- Describe what you would do if you visited this environment.

Life and Earth Science: Plants and Animals Change Their Environments

Investigate: Check for Clues

Take a walk around your neighborhood. Look for clues that show how animals and plants change their environment. Can you find these clues? Check off each you see on your walk.

☐ a plant growing out of a crack

☐ a leaf nibbled by insects

☐ grass growing out of a curb

☐ a tree root breaking a sidewalk or road

☐ wood or bark chewed by insects

TALK ABOUT IT!
- What other nature clues might you find on a walk?
- Did you find clues that puzzled you? How could you find out what made them?

Life and Earth Science: Plants and Animals Change Their Environments

Sort It Out

Not all trash is garbage! Circle the things that can be recycled to make new objects. Cross off the things that can be composted to make soil for a garden.

Recycling is using old materials to make new objects. **Composting** is using old leaves and food scraps to make soil.

This fleece jacket was made from recycled plastic bottles!

TALK ABOUT IT!
- How did you decide which objects to circle and which objects to cross off?
- What other things do you think you can recycle?
- What other things can you compost?

Life and Earth Science: People Affect Their Environments

Clean It Up!

Yuck! This park was messy. But people are working to clean it up. Can you find these pictures in the scene?

- ☐ a person sweeping with a broom
- ☐ a person raking leaves
- ☐ a person dragging a garbage bag
- ☐ an old newspaper
- ☐ an apple core

TALK ABOUT IT!
- Describe how you would help to clean up a park or a beach.
- What supplies do you think you would need?

Life and Earth Science: People Affect Their Environments

Create: Recycled-Paper Collage

YOU NEED:
- paper that is ready to be recycled, such as old magazines, paper bags, used greeting cards, and used wrapping paper • scissors • glue

1. Pick the largest piece of paper. Use it as your background.
2. Cut or tear shapes out of the other pieces of paper.
3. Glue them all over the background.
4. Hang up your collage for everybody to enjoy.

A collage is a picture or design made by attaching bits of paper or other materials to a background.

TALK ABOUT IT!
- Most paper is made from trees. Why do you think reusing and recycling paper helps forests?
- How can you avoid wasting paper? What are some other ways that you can reuse old paper?

Life and Earth Science: People Affect Their Environments

Investigate: Mop Up an Oil Spill

YOU NEED:
- spoon
- vegetable oil or olive oil
- glass of water
- cotton balls

1. Put a spoonful of oil into the water. Stir.
2. Watch the glass for a few minutes. What happens?
3. Dab the oil with a cotton ball. What happens?
4. See how much oil you can remove using cotton balls.

An oil tanker is a ship that carries a load of oil. If a tanker spills oil, people must work hard to clean up the mess.

TALK ABOUT IT!
- Describe what happened in the glass of water after you stirred oil into it. What did the oil do?
- Describe what happened when you dabbed the oil with a cotton ball. What other materials could you use to soak up the oil?

Life and Earth Science: People Affect Their Environments

What Will You Wear?

Circle the clothes you wear on a warm day. Cross off the clothes you wear on a cold day.

Draw yourself dressed for the weather on a warm, sunny day and on a snowy day.

TALK ABOUT IT!

Describe the weather where you live. Does the weather change with the seasons? Is it hot in the summer and cold in the winter? Is it hot all year long?

Earth Science: Weather

Drip, Drop, Splash

It's raining; it's pouring! Find and circle at least 12 differences between these pictures.

Clouds are made of tiny drops of water. The drops join to form bigger, heavy drops that fall as rain.

TALK ABOUT IT!
- Describe the rain where you live. Does it rain a lot or just a little?
- What do you like to do on a rainy day?

When the Wind Blows

A wind sock moves when the wind blows. It shows how fast the wind is blowing. The faster the wind, the higher the wind sock moves!

Which wind sock below shows a fast wind? Circle it. Which wind sock shows no wind? Cross it off. Look at the wind sock that you didn't circle or cross off. What does it tell you about the wind?

All airports have **wind socks**. The wind socks help pilots see how fast the wind is blowing and what direction it's blowing from.

Think about a kite that you would like to fly on a windy day. Draw it here. Try to build your kite using items found around the house, and see if it flies.

TALK ABOUT IT!
- Describe a windy day. How does wind feel?
- What things can a gentle wind move as it blows? What about a strong wind?

Earth Science: Weather

Investigate:
Snow Show

Make a snowflake viewer.

YOU NEED:
- scissors • black felt • cardboard
- glue • magnifying glass

Snowflakes are crystals made of ice. Every snowflake has 6 sides or points.

1. Cut out a rectangle of black felt.
2. Glue it to a piece of cardboard.
3. Put it in the freezer and wait for a snowy day.
4. Take your viewer outside and collect snowflakes on the black felt.
5. Use a magnifying glass to look at the details of the snowflakes.

No two large snowflakes are exactly alike in nature. But each snowflake on this page has an exact match! Draw lines to match the identical pairs.

TALK ABOUT IT!
- How does it feel outside when it's snowing?
- What happens to snow when the weather gets warmer?

Earth Science: Weather

Whoosh!

The snow is just right for a snowboarding contest. Follow each path to see which place each snowboarder comes in.

The temperature drops as you go up a mountain. Very tall mountains can be covered with snow all year.

1st 2nd 3rd 4th

TALK ABOUT IT!
- What would you like to do outside on a snowy day?
- What can you build with snow?

Earth Science: Weather

A Year of Weather

TALK ABOUT IT!
- What is your favorite season—spring, summer, fall, or winter?
- Which season is shown in each picture above? How do you know?

Investigate: Track the Weather

Keep track of the weather where you live for a week. Use this calendar. Draw or write about the weather every day.

Weather scientists keep track of weather over time. They look for **patterns**.

Day 1	Day 2	Day 3

Day 4	Day 5	Day 6	Day 7

TALK ABOUT IT!
- How many cloudy days did you record? How many sunny days?
- Were there any windy days?
- Can you find any patterns?
- Predict what your calendar might look like if you kept track of the weather in a different season.

Earth Science: Weather

Create: Show the Weather

Make weather pictures to show what the weather is like each day.

> **YOU NEED:**
> • markers or crayons • white paper
> • scissors • small magnet

1. Draw a sun, clouds, rain, snow, and a flag blowing in the wind.
2. Cut out your drawings.
3. Check the weather every day. Pick the picture that best shows the day's weather.
4. Use a magnet to put your picture on the refrigerator or other metal surface.

TALK ABOUT IT!
- What is your favorite kind of weather?
- Tell about a time you looked out the window and were surprised by the weather.
- What other kinds of weather could you draw pictures of?

Hurricane Alert

A hurricane can knock down trees and make the power go out.

A **hurricane** is a storm with heavy rain and powerful winds.

People stock up on useful items when a big storm is coming. Circle the items that are important to have on hand in a storm. Cross off the things that would not be important.

TALK ABOUT IT!
- What else could you do to prepare for a storm?
- What kinds of storms happen where you live? Describe a big storm you have experienced.

Earth Science: Extreme Weather

Hold On to Your Hats!

Gray clouds! Gusty winds! A storm is on its way. Time to go inside!

It's important to go inside if you see **lightning** or hear **thunder**. Even just being inside a car will help keep you safe.

Many people in this town are hurrying home. See if you can spot **10** hats and other headwear before they blow away.

TALK ABOUT IT!
- How can you tell a storm is coming?
- How do you think wild animals stay safe during a big storm?

Investigate: Staying Dry

Materials that keep out water are waterproof.

Find out which materials would keep you dry in a heavy rainstorm.

YOU NEED:
- 4 cotton balls • 4 clear glass jars • materials, such as a paper towel, a square of aluminum foil, a plastic sandwich bag, a facecloth
- scissors • tape • plastic bin • measuring cup filled with water

1. Put a cotton ball in each jar.
2. Place one of your material squares on top of each jar.
3. Tape the material to hold it onto the jar.
4. Put all the jars into the plastic bin.
5. Predict what you think will happen to each material. Then slowly pour a little water onto the material covering each jar. Watch what happens.
6. Touch the materials. How do they feel? Observe the cotton ball in each jar. What do you see?

TALK ABOUT IT!
- What did you find out? Were your predictions correct? What surprised you?
- Test other materials. Compare the materials to how your own raincoat looks and feels.

Earth Science: Extreme Weather

It's Only Natural!

Circle the pictures that show things you can find in nature. Cross off the things that people have made.

> A **natural resource** is something found in nature that people use to live and to make things.

TALK ABOUT IT!
- Describe how you sorted out the pictures.
- What are the things made by people used for? What do you think they are made from?

Water Power!

This is the Hoover Dam in the western United States. It uses the Colorado River's running water to make electricity. People can also get drinking water from the river. Can you find the **9** objects in this Hidden Pictures puzzle?

The water behind the Hoover Dam forms a lake called Lake Mead. It is one of the world's biggest lakes made by people.

 ruler

 lock

 paper clip

 cookie

 banana

 ice-cream cone

 hand rake

 sailboat

TALK ABOUT IT!
- What do you think this dam is made of?
- How do you think running water is used to make electricity?
- What other natural resources can you find in the picture?

Earth Science: Natural Resources

Investigate: Household Hunt

Your home and the objects in it are made from materials found in nature. Look around your home. Can you find objects made from these natural resources?

- ☐ metal
- ☐ wood
- ☐ glass
- ☐ stone
- ☐ rubber
- ☐ wool

Glass is made from sand. Most plastic is made from oil, but some plastic is made from corn.

TALK ABOUT IT!
- What natural resources do you think were used to build your home? Your furniture? Your clothes?
- Can you find objects that are made of many materials?

 Invent:
Reuse a Milk Jug

Look at all these things that were made from old, empty milk jugs. What do you think each of these inventions is used for?

Recycled milk jugs are made into new plastic objects, such as lumber and chairs.

Now it's your turn. Design a new use for an empty milk jug.

1. Make a plan. Draw a picture that shows your design.
2. Follow your plan to make your invention. Ask an adult for help if your plan requires cutting the milk jug with scissors.
3. Share your invention with an adult. Describe how it is used.

Earth Science: Natural Resources

Highlights

Congratulations!

_____
(your name)

worked hard
and finished the
Hands-On
STEAM
Learning Fun Workbook

Glossary

absorb soak up

cloud a white or gray mass of tiny water drops, which join to form bigger, heavy drops that fall as rain

collage a picture or design made by attaching bits of paper or other materials to a background

composting using old leaves and food scraps to make soil

environment all the living and nonliving things in an area

force a push or a pull that happens when 2 objects interact

freeze to take away so much heat that a liquid turns into a solid

habitat a place where animals and plants live in the wild

heavy having much weight

hurricane a storm with heavy rain and very strong winds

ice frozen water; the solid form of water

light having little weight

lightning natural electricity from thunderclouds; appears as a bright flash in the sky

melt to add so much heat that a solid turns into a liquid

natural resource something found in nature that people use to live and to make things

need something that a plant or an animal must have to live

observe to use the 5 senses to get information from the environment

pattern something that repeats over and over again

predict to say in advance that something is going to happen

pull to move something closer

push to move something away

recycling using old materials to make new objects

season a time of year that has a certain pattern of weather

snowflakes crystals made of ice

temperature the measurement of how hot or cold something is

thunder the rumble that follows a flash of lightning

waterproof describes a material that keeps out water

weather what the air is like outside; includes sunshine, clouds, temperature, and rain, snow, sleet, or hail

wind moving air

wind sock a cloth tube that moves when the wind blows to show the speed and direction of the wind

Answers

Page 4
Move It!

Page 5
Pull Hard!

Page 8
Puppet Pulls

Page 9
Sun Power
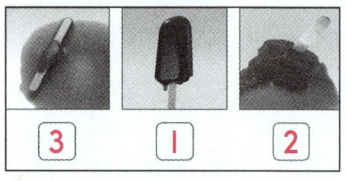

Page 11
Hot and Cold
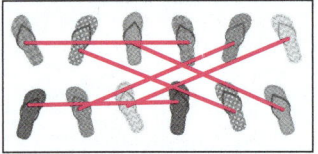

Page 16
Grow, Seeds, Grow!

Page 17
Wild Wonders

Page 14
Time to Eat
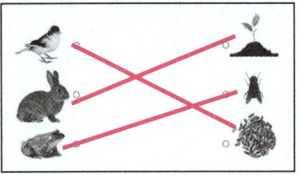

Page 19
Plant Power

Page 20
Acorns to Oaks
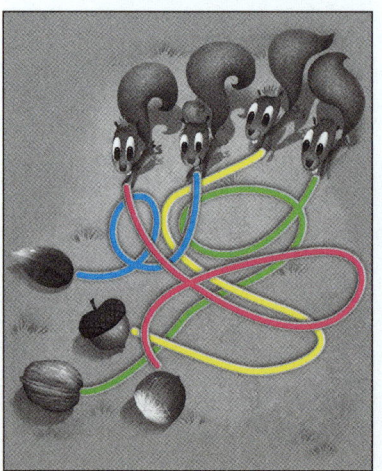

Page 22
At Home in Holes

Page 25
Sort It Out

Answers

Page 26
Clean It Up!

Page 30
Drip, Drop, Splash

Page 32
Snow Show
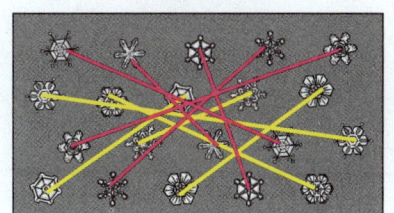

Page 33
Whoosh!

Page 34
A Year of Weather

Page 37
Hurricane Alert

Page 38
Hold On to Your Hats!

Page 40
It's Only Natural!

Page 41
Water Power!
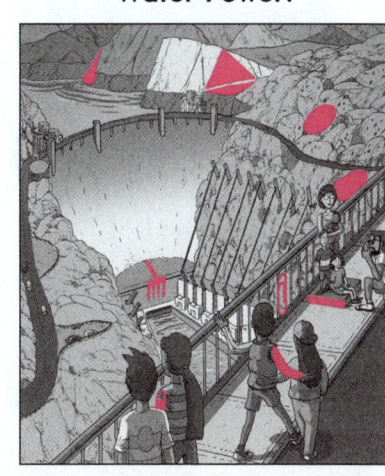

Extend the Learning

Want to explore further? Encourage your child's interest and curiosity in the topics throughout the book. Here are some ideas to get you started.

Force and Motion *(pages 2–8)*

Every force can be described as a push or a pull. Go on a hunt with your child to identify objects that can be pushed or pulled or both. Get out some toy cars and guide your child to test out some ideas. Talk about these questions: *How can you change how fast or how far a car moves? How can you change its direction? How can you make a moving car stop moving?*

Energy: Effects of the Sun *(pages 9–13)*

Take a walk with your child on a warm, sunny day. Look for evidence of the sun's warmth. Talk about these questions: *Can you feel the warmth on your skin? Is the sidewalk warm? If you had ice cream, what would happen to it?* Then talk about how to stay cool in the sun. Encourage your child to find shady places and use the senses to tell whether they are cooler than sunny places.

Needs of Living Things *(pages 14–18)*

Living things need different kinds of food to meet their needs. Ask your child to talk about the foods your family eats. Then discuss foods other animals eat, such as dogs/dog food, squirrels/acorns, and cows/grass. Go on to explain that plants make their own food. Have your child point out plants in your home and outdoors. Discuss: *What do plants need to live and grow? What happens to plants when they do not get what they need? How do you know?*

Plants and Animals Change Their Environments *(pages 19–24)*

Explore the environment near your home with your child. Take a nature walk in your yard or a local park. What animals and plants can you find? Can you spot any nests or other animal homes? You may wish to use the camera on your cell phone to take photos and use its voice recorder to tell about what you see. When you get home, work with your child to use the photos and voice recordings to make a slide show.